CLASSICAL GREATS
Playalong *for* Trumpet

Amsco Publications
A Part of **The Music Sales Group**
New York/Nashville/Los Angeles/London/Paris/Sydney/Copenhagen/Berlin/Tokyo/Madrid

Cover photography: George Taylor
Project editor: Heather Ramage

Order No. AM 988526
ISBN-10: 0.8256.3519.5
ISBN-13: 978.0.8256.3519.9

Exclusive Distributors:
Music Sales Corporation
257 Park Avenue South, New York, NY 10010 USA
Music Sales Limited
14-15 Berners Street, London W1T 3LJ England
Music Sales Pty. Limited
120 Rothschild Street, Rosebery, Sydney, NSW 2018, Australia

Printed in the United States of America

Center Stage

Trumpet Fingering Chart

MOUTHPIECE

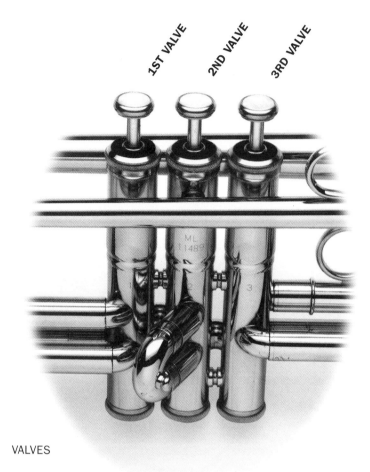

VALVES

1ST VALVE 2ND VALVE 3RD VALVE

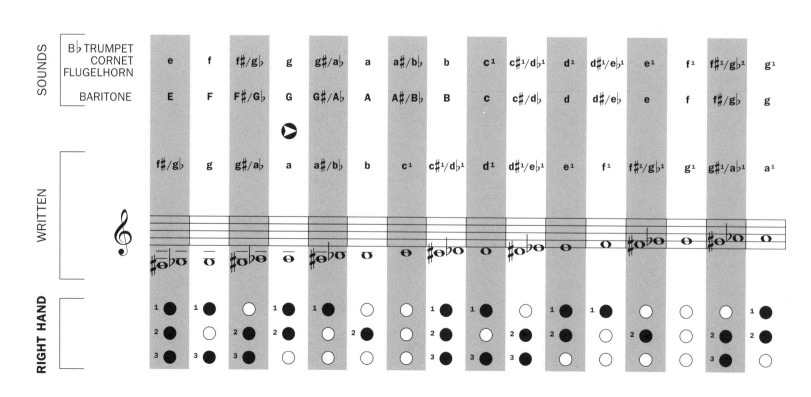

Indicates the lower limit of the best playing range

Transposition

The B♭ trumpet, cornet and flugelhorn
sound a major second below the written pitch.
Rule: **Written C sounds B♭**

Written:    Sounds:

The baritone sounds a major ninth below
the written pitch. Rule: **Written C sounds B♭**

Written:    Sounds:

Pitch System

The letter names which appear at the top of the
fingering chart indicate the relative octave as well as
the name of each pitch, as shown below.

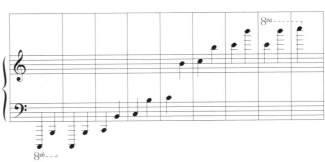

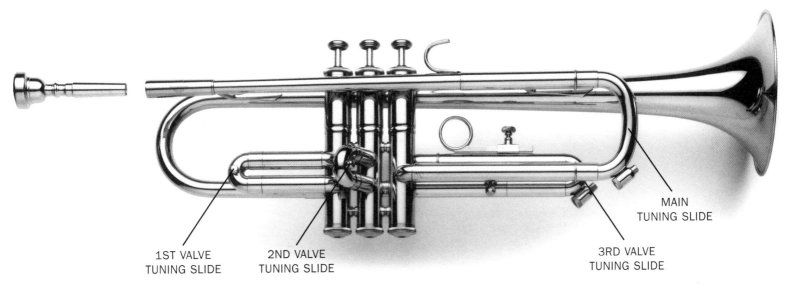

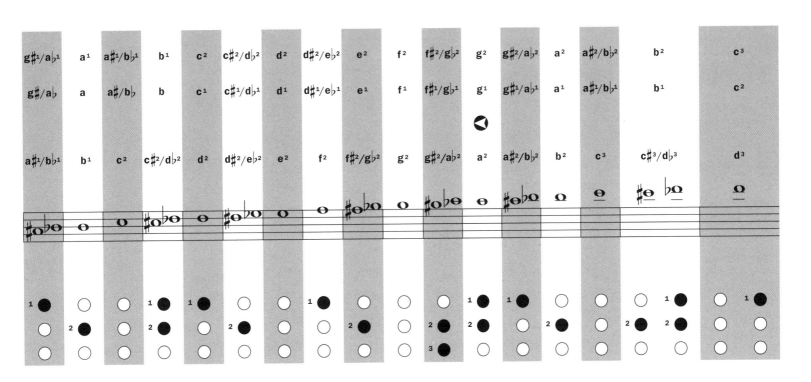

⬕ Indicates the upper limit of the best playing range

Air (from *The Water Music*)

Composed by George Frideric Handel

Habañera (from *Carmen*)

Composed by Georges Bizet

CD Track

2

Andantino

0:07

0:32

Jesu, Joy Of Man's Desiring

Composed by Johann Sebastian Bach

Jupiter (from *The Planets Suite*)

Composed by Gustav Holst

Andante maestoso

0:09

0:25

0:41

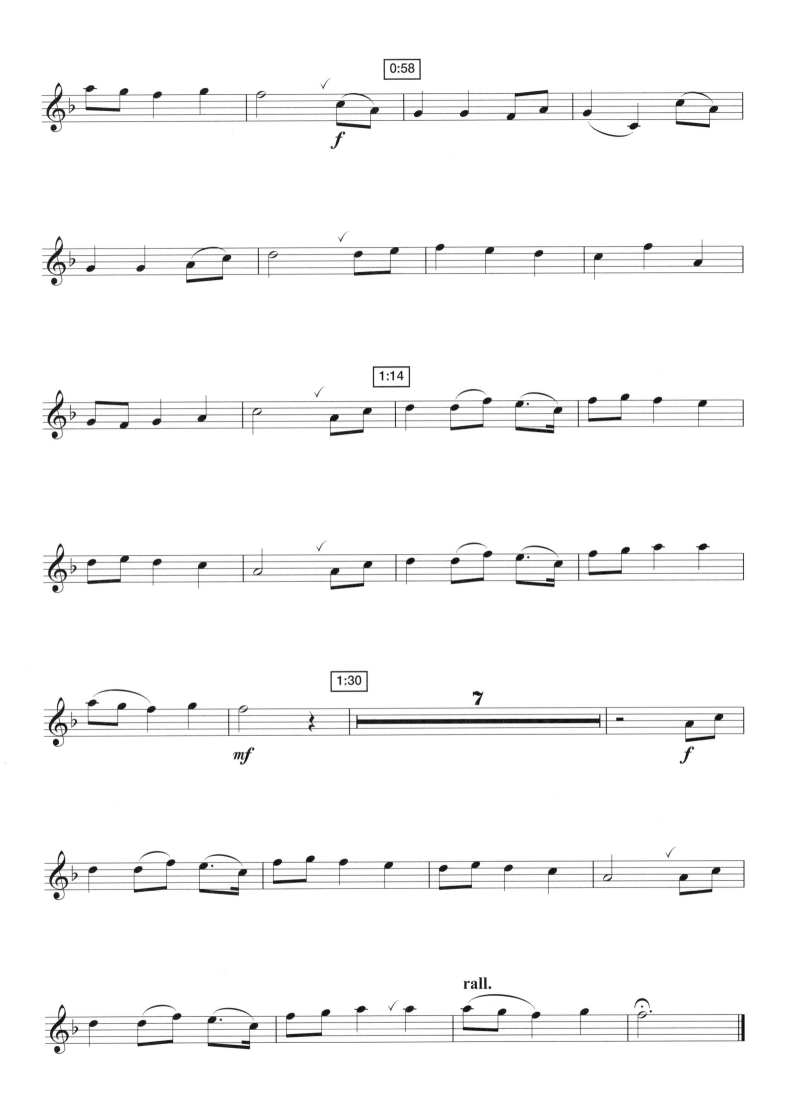

The New World Symphony (Theme)

Composed by Antonín Dvořák

Largo

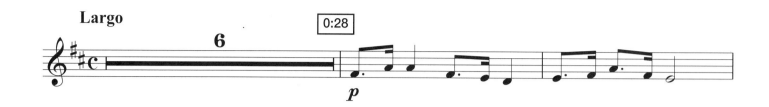

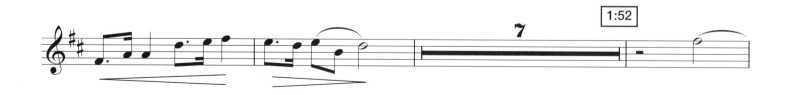

2:36

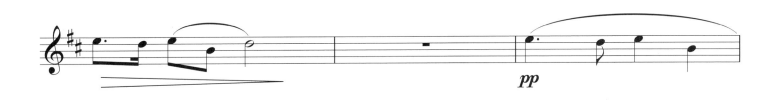

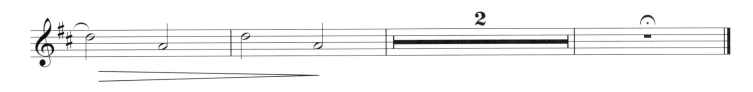

March (from *The Nutcracker Suite*)

Composed by Pyotr Ilyich Tchaikovsky

Air On The "G" String

Composed by Johann Sebastian Bach

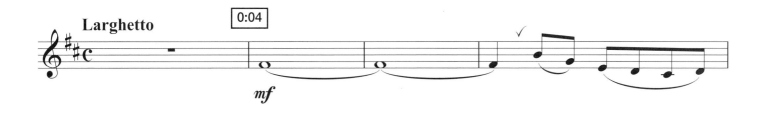

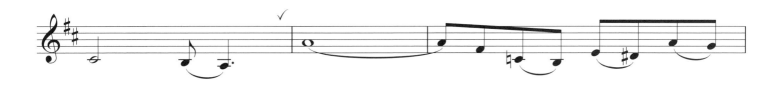

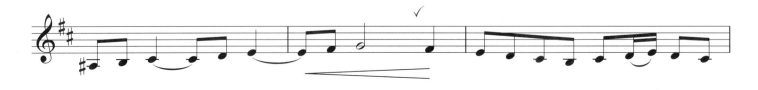

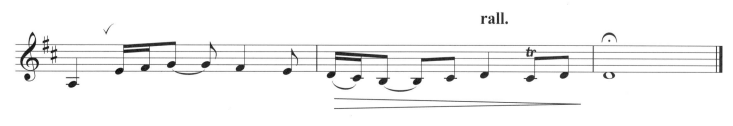

Ode To Joy
(Theme from *Symphony No.9* "Choral")

Composed by Ludwig van Beethoven

CD Track
8

Allegro

O For The Wings Of A Dove

Composed by Felix Mendelssohn

Spring (from *The Four Seasons*)

Composed by Antonio Vivaldi

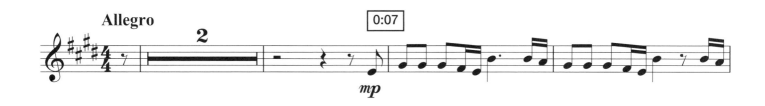

Note: To help you keep your place in each song, timing markers, which correspond to the audio CD, have been included. They appear in a box at regular points in the music, e.g., 1:37

Also Available *on*

CenterStage

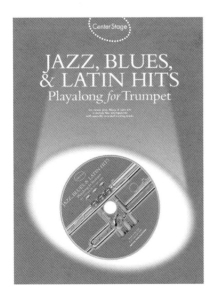

JAZZ, BLUES, & LATIN HITS
Playalong for Trumpet

Includes ten well-known hits with a specially recorded backing track CD: Cry Me A River, Guantanamera, Fly Me To The Moon (In Other Words), Hit The Road Jack, I Wish I Knew How It Would Feel To Be Free, Li'l Darlin', Opus One, Perdido, Desafinado (Slightly Out Of Tune), Take The "A" Train

Order No. AM987327